I0541778

TABLE OF CONTENTS

Copyright © 2023 by Dr. Bob E. Neal
All rights reserved. ISBN: 979-8-9861038-5-3
Published by Along the Way, LLC.

No part of this booklet including icons and images may be reproduced in any form without prior written permission from the author, except noted in the text and in the case of brief quotations embodied in cited articles and studies. Unless otherwise noted, all Scripture quotations are from the English Standard Version (ESV) and are used with permission under the Gratis Use Policy.

HOW TO USE THIS READING PLAN

This Bible Reading Plan is a 23-week chronological reading of all four Gospels exploring the birth, life, death, resurrection, and ascension of Jesus the Messiah. Each week is presented with several passages of Scripture revolving around one unique theme that emerges from Jesus' life as seen in the writings of Matthew, Mark, Luke, and John. These stories are based on a condensed timeline of the entirety of Jesus' life from His birth on earth to His ascension into Heaven.

The three criteria that went into the development of this reading plan are:
- **Chronology** – The recorded events in the timeline of Jesus' life on earth.
- **Theme** – Some of the big ideas or "headlines" that emerge from those recorded events.
- **Harmony** – A synthesis of Scriptural passages from all four Gospels where those events are referenced.

This 23-week devotional is organized as a 3-volume set. Volume 1 is eight weeks long and covers the early years of the life of Jesus. Volume 2 covers the middle years of Jesus' public ministry over seven weeks. Volume 3 covers the final years of Jesus' public ministry and is eight weeks.

Our desire is that as you read the story of Jesus through the Gospels, His life unfolds before you like a binge-worthy drama that connects historical chronology to patterns of our everyday lives. Ultimately, our prayer is for you to experience first-hand the living, resurrected Messiah King Jesus as the Chief Shepherd of your soul (1 Peter 2:25).

DAILY DEVOTIONAL AND JOURNAL

DAY 1

Feel free to journal about some of the things you feel like the Lord is doing in your life. You may also desire to bring this journal with you to a weekend worship experience and take notes on the sermon/message. During Days 2-6, we recommend you use the P.R.A.Y. Method:

DAY 2-6

Pray – Praying with Jesus. Begin your time of devotion with prayer. Use this pattern for prayer inspired by The Lord's Prayer (Matthew 6:5-15; Luke 11:1-13)

- **Praise** (*"Our Father, who is in Heaven..."*). Thank God for who He is and praise Him for the things He has done in your life.
- **Petitions** (*"Let Your Kingdom come..."*). Ask the Lord for specific things to be done in the world, your life, and in the lives of others.
- **Proclamations** (*"Yours is the Kingdom and the Power and the Glory..."*). End your time of prayer with a proclamation of God's rule, reign, and sovereignty.

Read – Reading about Jesus. Write about verses that stand out as you go through the Gospel readings. As you read, try to keep a few questions in mind:
- Who is speaking?
- Who is being spoken to?
- What could this potentially mean for my life today?

Ask – Asking for guidance from Jesus. Spend time asking the Lord for wisdom and insight as you meditate on what you prayed and the Scriptures you read. A good practice is to ask the Holy Spirit — who Jesus promised would "teach you all things" (John 14:26) — to teach you something about the life of Jesus that day.

Yield – Yielding our will to Jesus. Take time throughout your day to intentionally yield to the Lord and demonstrate Christ-likeness in your daily life. Write out some ways you are becoming like Jesus each day.

DAY 7

Day 7 ends with a time of Sabbath rest, reflection, and the opportunity to catch up on any missed readings from that week.

OVERVIEW OF THE WEEKLY READINGS FROM "23" VOLUME 2

OUR PRAYER FOR YOU AS YOU ENGAGE IN THIS DAILY JOURNEY WITH JESUS THROUGH THE GOSPELS:

SPEND TIME WITH JESUS

LEARN FROM JESUS

BECOME MORE LIKE JESUS

WEEK: 1

WEEK: 1	WEEKLY MEMORY VERSE:
	"And he answered, "You shall love the Lord your God with all your heart and with all your soul and with all your strength and with all your mind, and your neighbor as yourself." - **Luke 10:27**

TODAY'S READING:

Luke 10:25-42
Matthew 12:1-49

PRAY: Take time to bring praise, petitions and/or proclamations to the Lord today.

READ: What are some Scriptures or stories that stood out to you today?

ASK: What's something the Holy Spirit wants you to learn about Jesus today?

YIELD: What are some ways that you can (or did) yield to the Lord today?

WEEK: 1	WEEKLY MEMORY VERSE:
	"And he answered, "You shall love the Lord your God with all your heart and with all your soul and with all your strength and with all your mind, and your neighbor as yourself." - **Luke 10:27**
TODAY'S READING: **Matthew 13:1-58**	

PRAY: Take time to bring praise, petitions and/or proclamations to the Lord today.

READ: What are some Scriptures or stories that stood out to you today?

ASK: What's something the Holy Spirit wants you to learn about Jesus today?

YIELD: What are some ways that you can (or did) yield to the Lord today?

WEEK: 1	WEEKLY MEMORY VERSE:
	"And he answered, "You shall love the Lord your God with all your heart and with all your soul and with all your strength and with all your mind, and your neighbor as yourself." - **Luke 10:27**
TODAY'S READING: John 4:1-54	

PRAY: Take time to bring praise, petitions and/or proclamations to the Lord today.

READ: What are some Scriptures or stories that stood out to you today?

ASK: What's something the Holy Spirit wants you to learn about Jesus today?

YIELD: What are some ways that you can (or did) yield to the Lord today?

WEEK: 1	WEEKLY MEMORY VERSE:
TODAY'S READING: # John 5:1-47	*"And he answered, "You shall love the Lord your God with all your heart and with all your soul and with all your strength and with all your mind, and your neighbor as yourself." -* **Luke 10:27**

PRAY: Take time to bring praise, petitions and/or proclamations to the Lord today.

READ: What are some Scriptures or stories that stood out to you today?

ASK: What's something the Holy Spirit wants you to learn about Jesus today?

YIELD: What are some ways that you can (or did) yield to the Lord today?

WEEK: 1	WEEKLY MEMORY VERSE:
	"And he answered, "You shall love the Lord your God with all your heart and with all your soul and with all your strength and with all your mind, and your neighbor as yourself." - **Luke 10:27**
TODAY'S READING: ## Mark 5:1-43	

PRAY: Take time to bring praise, petitions and/or proclamations to the Lord today.

READ: What are some Scriptures or stories that stood out to you today?

ASK: What's something the Holy Spirit wants you to learn about Jesus today?

YIELD: What are some ways that you can (or did) yield to the Lord today?

WEEK: 1	WEEKLY MEMORY VERSE:
RECAP OF WEEK 1 SCRIPTURES: Mon - Luke 10:25-42; Matthew 12:1-49 Tues - Matthew 13:1-58 Wed - John 4:1-54 Thur - John 5:1-47 Fri - Mark 5:1-43	*"And he answered, "You shall love the Lord your God with all your heart and with all your soul and with all your strength and with all your mind, and your neighbor as yourself."* - **Luke 10:27**

REST: What are some ways that I can rest in the Lord today?

REFLECT: What are some things that I learned about the life of Jesus—and myself—this week?

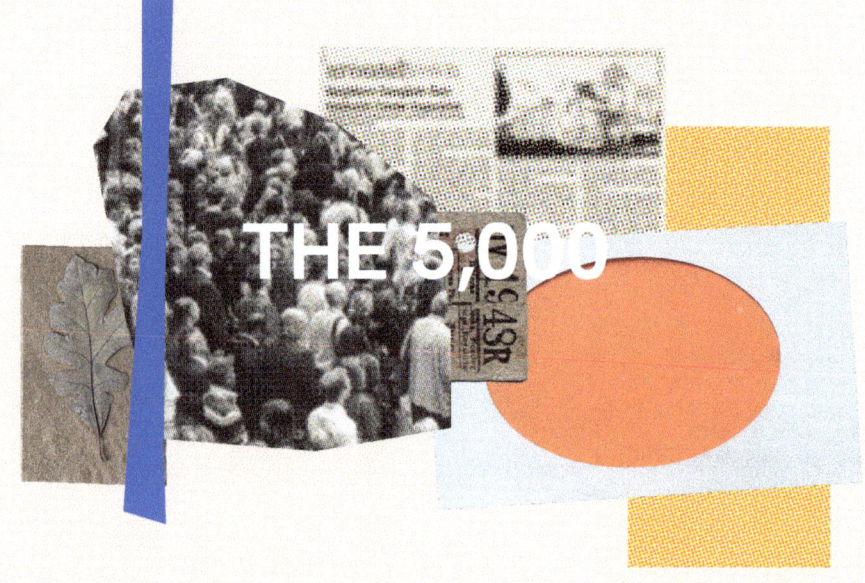

THE 5,000

WEEK: 2	**WEEKLY MEMORY VERSE:**
	"When he went ashore he saw a great crowd, and he had compassion on them, becuase they were like sheep without a shepherd. And he began to teach them many things." - **Mark 6:34**
TODAY'S READING: Mark 6:1-56	

PRAY: Take time to bring praise, petitions and/or proclamations to the Lord today.

READ: What are some Scriptures or stories that stood out to you today?

ASK: What's something the Holy Spirit wants you to learn about Jesus today?

YIELD: What are some ways that you can (or did) yield to the Lord today?

WEEK: 2	WEEKLY MEMORY VERSE:
	*"When he went ashore he saw a great crowd, and he had compassion on them, becuase they were like sheep without a shepherd. And he began to teach them many things." - **Mark 6:34***
TODAY'S READING: John 6:1-21	

PRAY: Take time to bring praise, petitions and/or proclamations to the Lord today.

READ: What are some Scriptures or stories that stood out to you today?

ASK: What's something the Holy Spirit wants you to learn about Jesus today?

YIELD: What are some ways that you can (or did) yield to the Lord today?

WEEK: 2	WEEKLY MEMORY VERSE:
	"When he went ashore he saw a great crowd, and he had compassion on them, becuase they were like sheep without a shepherd. And he began to teach them many things." - **Mark 6:34**
TODAY'S READING: **John 6:22-71**	

PRAY: Take time to bring praise, petitions and/or proclamations to the Lord today.

READ: What are some Scriptures or stories that stood out to you today?

ASK: What's something the Holy Spirit wants you to learn about Jesus today?

YIELD: What are some ways that you can (or did) yield to the Lord today?

WEEK: 2	WEEKLY MEMORY VERSE:
	"When he went ashore he saw a great crowd, and he had compassion on them, becuase they were like sheep without a shepherd. And he began to teach them many things." - **Mark 6:34**
TODAY'S READING: # Matthew 14:1-36	

PRAY: Take time to bring praise, petitions and/or proclamations to the Lord today.

READ: What are some Scriptures or stories that stood out to you today?

ASK: What's something the Holy Spirit wants you to learn about Jesus today?

YIELD: What are some ways that you can (or did) yield to the Lord today?

WEEK: 2	WEEKLY MEMORY VERSE:
	"When he went ashore he saw a great crowd, and he had compassion on them, becuase they were like sheep without a shepherd. And he began to teach them many things." - **Mark 6:34**
TODAY'S READING: Luke 11:1-54	

PRAY: Take time to bring praise, petitions and/or proclamations to the Lord today.

READ: What are some Scriptures or stories that stood out to you today?

ASK: What's something the Holy Spirit wants you to learn about Jesus today?

YIELD: What are some ways that you can (or did) yield to the Lord today?

WEEK: 2	WEEKLY MEMORY VERSE:
	"When he went ashore he saw a great crowd, and he had compassion on them, becuase they were like sheep without a shepherd. And he began to teach them many things." - **Mark 6:34**
RECAP OF WEEK 2 SCRIPTURES: Mon - Mark 6:1-56 Tues - John 6:1-21 Wed - John 6:22-71 Thur - Matthew 14:1-36 Fri - Luke 11:1-54	

REST: What are some ways that I can rest in the Lord today?

REFLECT: What are some things that I learned about the life of Jesus—and myself—this week?

TRADITIONS

WEEK: 3	WEEKLY MEMORY VERSE:
	"But what comes out of the mouth proceeds from the heart, and this defiles a person." - Matthew 15:18
TODAY'S READING: ## Matthew 15:1-39	

PRAY: Take time to bring praise, petitions and/or proclamations to the Lord today.

READ: What are some Scriptures or stories that stood out to you today?

ASK: What's something the Holy Spirit wants you to learn about Jesus today?

YIELD: What are some ways that you can (or did) yield to the Lord today?

WEEK: 3	WEEKLY MEMORY VERSE:
	*"But what comes out of the mouth proceeds from the heart, and this defiles a person." - **Matthew 15:18****
TODAY'S READING:	
# Mark 7:1-37	

PRAY: Take time to bring praise, petitions and/or proclamations to the Lord today.

READ: What are some Scriptures or stories that stood out to you today?

ASK: What's something the Holy Spirit wants you to learn about Jesus today?

YIELD: What are some ways that you can (or did) yield to the Lord today?

WEEK: 3	WEEKLY MEMORY VERSE:
	"But what comes out of the mouth proceeds from the heart, and this defiles a person." - **Matthew 15:18**
TODAY'S READING: Luke 12:1-34	

PRAY: Take time to bring praise, petitions and/or proclamations to the Lord today.

READ: What are some Scriptures or stories that stood out to you today?

ASK: What's something the Holy Spirit wants you to learn about Jesus today?

YIELD: What are some ways that you can (or did) yield to the Lord today?

WEEK: 3	WEEKLY MEMORY VERSE:
	"But what comes out of the mouth proceeds from the heart, and this defiles a person." - **Matthew 15:18**
TODAY'S READING:	
# Luke 12:35-59	

PRAY: Take time to bring praise, petitions and/or proclamations to the Lord today.

READ: What are some Scriptures or stories that stood out to you today?

ASK: What's something the Holy Spirit wants you to learn about Jesus today?

YIELD: What are some ways that you can (or did) yield to the Lord today?

WEEK: 3	WEEKLY MEMORY VERSE:
	"But what comes out of the mouth proceeds from the heart, and this defiles a person." - **Matthew 15:18**
TODAY'S READING: # John 7:1-52	

PRAY: Take time to bring praise, petitions and/or proclamations to the Lord today.

READ: What are some Scriptures or stories that stood out to you today?

ASK: What's something the Holy Spirit wants you to learn about Jesus today?

YIELD: What are some ways that you can (or did) yield to the Lord today?

WEEK: 3	WEEKLY MEMORY VERSE:
	"But what comes out of the mouth proceeds from the heart, and this defiles a person." - **Matthew 15:18**
RECAP OF WEEK 3 SCRIPTURES: Mon - Matthew 15:1-39 Tues - Mark 7:1-37 Wed - Luke 12:1-34 Thur - Luke 12:35-59 Fri - John 7:1-52	

REST: What are some ways that I can rest in the Lord today?

REFLECT: What are some things that I learned about the life of Jesus—and myself—this week?

THE CONFESSION

WEEK: 4	WEEKLY MEMORY VERSE:
	*And he asked them, "But who do you say that I am?" Peter answered him, "You are the Christ." - **Mark 8:29***
TODAY'S READING:	
# Mark 8:1-38 Matthew 16:1-20	

PRAY: Take time to bring praise, petitions and/or proclamations to the Lord today.

READ: What are some Scriptures or stories that stood out to you today?

ASK: What's something the Holy Spirit wants you to learn about Jesus today?

YIELD: What are some ways that you can (or did) yield to the Lord today?

WEEK: 4	WEEKLY MEMORY VERSE:
	*And he asked them, "But who do you say that I am?" Peter answered him, "You are the Christ." - **Mark 8:29***

TODAY'S READING:

Matthew 16:21-28
Matthew 17:1-27

PRAY: Take time to bring praise, petitions and/or proclamations to the Lord today.

READ: What are some Scriptures or stories that stood out to you today?

ASK: What's something the Holy Spirit wants you to learn about Jesus today?

YIELD: What are some ways that you can (or did) yield to the Lord today?

WEEK: 4	WEEKLY MEMORY VERSE:
	*And he asked them, "But who do you say that I am?" Peter answered him, "You are the Christ." - **Mark 8:29****
TODAY'S READING: Luke 13:1-35	

PRAY: Take time to bring praise, petitions and/or proclamations to the Lord today.

READ: What are some Scriptures or stories that stood out to you today?

ASK: What's something the Holy Spirit wants you to learn about Jesus today?

YIELD: What are some ways that you can (or did) yield to the Lord today?

WEEK: 4	WEEKLY MEMORY VERSE:
	*And he asked them, "But who do you say that I am?" Peter answered him, "You are the Christ." - **Mark 8:29***
TODAY'S READING: Luke 14:1-35	

PRAY: Take time to bring praise, petitions and/or proclamations to the Lord today.

READ: What are some Scriptures or stories that stood out to you today?

ASK: What's something the Holy Spirit wants you to learn about Jesus today?

YIELD: What are some ways that you can (or did) yield to the Lord today?

WEEK: 4	WEEKLY MEMORY VERSE:
	*And he asked them, "But who do you say that I am?" Peter answered him, "You are the Christ." - **Mark 8:29***
TODAY'S READING:	
John 8:1-59	

PRAY: Take time to bring praise, petitions and/or proclamations to the Lord today.

READ: What are some Scriptures or stories that stood out to you today?

ASK: What's something the Holy Spirit wants you to learn about Jesus today?

YIELD: What are some ways that you can (or did) yield to the Lord today?

WEEK: 4

RECAP OF WEEK 4 SCRIPTURES:
Mon - Mark 8:1-38; Matthew 16:1-20
Tues - Matthew 16:21-28; Matthew 17:1-27
Wed - Luke 13:1-35
Thur - Luke 14:1-35
    Fri - John 8:1-59

WEEKLY MEMORY VERSE:
And he asked them, "But who do you say that I am?" Peter answered him, "You are the Christ." - **Mark 8:29**

REST: What are some ways that I can rest in the Lord today?

REFLECT: What are some things that I learned about the life of Jesus—and myself—this week?

LOST AND FOUND

WEEK: 5	WEEKLY MEMORY VERSE:
	"And he arose and came to his father. But while he was still a long way off, his father saw him and felt compassion, and ran and embraced him and kissed him." - Luke 15:20
TODAY'S READING: **Luke 15:1-32**	

PRAY: Take time to bring praise, petitions and/or proclamations to the Lord today.

READ: What are some Scriptures or stories that stood out to you today?

ASK: What's something the Holy Spirit wants you to learn about Jesus today?

YIELD: What are some ways that you can (or did) yield to the Lord today?

WEEK: 5	WEEKLY MEMORY VERSE:
	"And he arose and came to his father. But while he was still a long way off, his father saw him and felt compassion, and ran and embraced him and kissed him." - **Luke 15:20**
TODAY'S READING: ## Matthew 18:1-35	

PRAY: Take time to bring praise, petitions and/or proclamations to the Lord today.

READ: What are some Scriptures or stories that stood out to you today?

ASK: What's something the Holy Spirit wants you to learn about Jesus today?

YIELD: What are some ways that you can (or did) yield to the Lord today?

WEEK: 5	WEEKLY MEMORY VERSE:
	"And he arose and came to his father. But while he was still a long way off, his father saw him and felt compassion, and ran and embraced him and kissed him." - **Luke 15:20**
TODAY'S READING:	
# Mark 9:1-50	

PRAY: Take time to bring praise, petitions and/or proclamations to the Lord today.

READ: What are some Scriptures or stories that stood out to you today?

ASK: What's something the Holy Spirit wants you to learn about Jesus today?

YIELD: What are some ways that you can (or did) yield to the Lord today?

WEEK: 5	WEEKLY MEMORY VERSE:
	"And he arose and came to his father. But while he was still a long way off, his father saw him and felt compassion, and ran and embraced him and kissed him." - **Luke 15:20**
TODAY'S READING: ## Mark 10:1-52	

PRAY: Take time to bring praise, petitions and/or proclamations to the Lord today.

READ: What are some Scriptures or stories that stood out to you today?

ASK: What's something the Holy Spirit wants you to learn about Jesus today?

YIELD: What are some ways that you can (or did) yield to the Lord today?

WEEK: 5	WEEKLY MEMORY VERSE:
	"And he arose and came to his father. But while he was still a long way off, his father saw him and felt compassion, and ran and embraced him and kissed him." - **Luke 15:20**
TODAY'S READING: # John 9:1-41	

PRAY: Take time to bring praise, petitions and/or proclamations to the Lord today.

READ: What are some Scriptures or stories that stood out to you today?

ASK: What's something the Holy Spirit wants you to learn about Jesus today?

YIELD: What are some ways that you can (or did) yield to the Lord today?

WEEK: 5	WEEKLY MEMORY VERSE:
	"And he arose and came to his father. But while he was still a long way off, his father saw him and felt compassion, and ran and embraced him and kissed him." - **Luke 15:20**
RECAP OF WEEK 5 SCRIPTURES:	
Mon - Luke 15:1-32	
Tues - Matthew 18:1-35	
Wed - Mark 9:1-50	
Thur - Mark 10:1-52	
Fri - John 9:1-41	

REST: What are some ways that I can rest in the Lord today?

REFLECT: What are some things that I learned about the life of Jesus—and myself—this week?

THE GOOD SHEPHERD

WEEK: 6	WEEKLY MEMORY VERSE:
	"My sheep hear my voice, and I know them, and they follow me." - **John 10:27**
TODAY'S READING:	
# John 10:1-42	

PRAY: Take time to bring praise, petitions and/or proclamations to the Lord today.

READ: What are some Scriptures or stories that stood out to you today?

ASK: What's something the Holy Spirit wants you to learn about Jesus today?

YIELD: What are some ways that you can (or did) yield to the Lord today?

PRAY: Take time to bring praise, petitions and/or proclamations to the Lord today.

READ: What are some Scriptures or stories that stood out to you today?

ASK: What's something the Holy Spirit wants you to learn about Jesus today?

YIELD: What are some ways that you can (or did) yield to the Lord today?

WEEK: 6	WEEKLY MEMORY VERSE:
	*"My sheep hear my voice, and I know them, and they follow me." - **John 10:27***
TODAY'S READING:	
# Mark 12:1-44	

PRAY: Take time to bring praise, petitions and/or proclamations to the Lord today.

READ: What are some Scriptures or stories that stood out to you today?

ASK: What's something the Holy Spirit wants you to learn about Jesus today?

YIELD: What are some ways that you can (or did) yield to the Lord today?

WEEK: 6	WEEKLY MEMORY VERSE:
	"My sheep hear my voice, and I know them, and they follow me." - **John 10:27**
TODAY'S READING:	
# Matthew 19:1-30	

PRAY: Take time to bring praise, petitions and/or proclamations to the Lord today.

READ: What are some Scriptures or stories that stood out to you today?

ASK: What's something the Holy Spirit wants you to learn about Jesus today?

YIELD: What are some ways that you can (or did) yield to the Lord today?

WEEK: 6	WEEKLY MEMORY VERSE:
	"My sheep hear my voice, and I know them, and they follow me." - **John 10:27**
TODAY'S READING: Luke 16:1-31	

PRAY: Take time to bring praise, petitions and/or proclamations to the Lord today.

READ: What are some Scriptures or stories that stood out to you today?

ASK: What's something the Holy Spirit wants you to learn about Jesus today?

YIELD: What are some ways that you can (or did) yield to the Lord today?

WEEK: 6	WEEKLY MEMORY VERSE:
	"My sheep hear my voice, and I know them, and they follow me." - **John 10:27**
RECAP OF WEEK 6 SCRIPTURES: Mon - John 10:1-42 Tues - Mark 11:1-33 Wed - Mark 12:1-44 Thur - Matthew 19:1-30 Fri - Luke 16:1-31	

REST: What are some ways that I can rest in the Lord today?

REFLECT: What are some things that I learned about the life of Jesus—and myself—this week?

THE RETURN

WEEK: 7

WEEK: 7	WEEKLY MEMORY VERSE:
	"Be on guard, keep awake. For you do not know when the time will come." - **Mark 13:33**
TODAY'S READING: # Mark 13:1-37	

PRAY: Take time to bring praise, petitions and/or proclamations to the Lord today.

READ: What are some Scriptures or stories that stood out to you today?

ASK: What's something the Holy Spirit wants you to learn about Jesus today?

YIELD: What are some ways that you can (or did) yield to the Lord today?

WEEK: 7	WEEKLY MEMORY VERSE:
	"Be on guard, keep awake. For you do not know when the time will come." - **Mark 13:33**
TODAY'S READING: # Luke 17:1-37	

PRAY: Take time to bring praise, petitions and/or proclamations to the Lord today.

READ: What are some Scriptures or stories that stood out to you today?

ASK: What's something the Holy Spirit wants you to learn about Jesus today?

YIELD: What are some ways that you can (or did) yield to the Lord today?

WEEK: 7	WEEKLY MEMORY VERSE:
	"Be on guard, keep awake. For you do not know when the time will come." - **Mark 13:33**
TODAY'S READING:	
# Matthew 20:1-34	

PRAY: Take time to bring praise, petitions and/or proclamations to the Lord today.

READ: What are some Scriptures or stories that stood out to you today?

ASK: What's something the Holy Spirit wants you to learn about Jesus today?

YIELD: What are some ways that you can (or did) yield to the Lord today?

WEEK: 7	WEEKLY MEMORY VERSE:
	"Be on guard, keep awake. For you do not know when the time will come." - **Mark 13:33**
TODAY'S READING:	
# John 11:1-57	

PRAY: Take time to bring praise, petitions and/or proclamations to the Lord today.

READ: What are some Scriptures or stories that stood out to you today?

ASK: What's something the Holy Spirit wants you to learn about Jesus today?

YIELD: What are some ways that you can (or did) yield to the Lord today?

WEEK: 7	WEEKLY MEMORY VERSE:
	"Be on guard, keep awake. For you do not know when the time will come." - **Mark 13:33**
TODAY'S READING:	
# Mark 14:1-72	

PRAY: Take time to bring praise, petitions and/or proclamations to the Lord today.

READ: What are some Scriptures or stories that stood out to you today?

ASK: What's something the Holy Spirit wants you to learn about Jesus today?

YIELD: What are some ways that you can (or did) yield to the Lord today?

WEEK: 7	WEEKLY MEMORY VERSE:
	"Be on guard, keep awake. For you do not know when the time will come." - **Mark 13:33**
RECAP OF WEEK 7 SCRIPTURES: Mon - Mark 13:1-37 Tues - Luke 17:1-37 Wed - Matthew 20:1-34 Thur - John 11:1-57 Fri - Mark 14:1-72	

REST: What are some ways that I can rest in the Lord today?

REFLECT: What are some things that I learned about the life of Jesus—and myself—this week?

COMING SOON
"23" VOLUME 3
THE FINAL YEARS

www.ingramcontent.com/pod-product-compliance
Lightning Source LLC
Chambersburg PA
CBHW051646120626
46551CB00015B/2244